The Human Body: Organs and Functions

# STOMACH

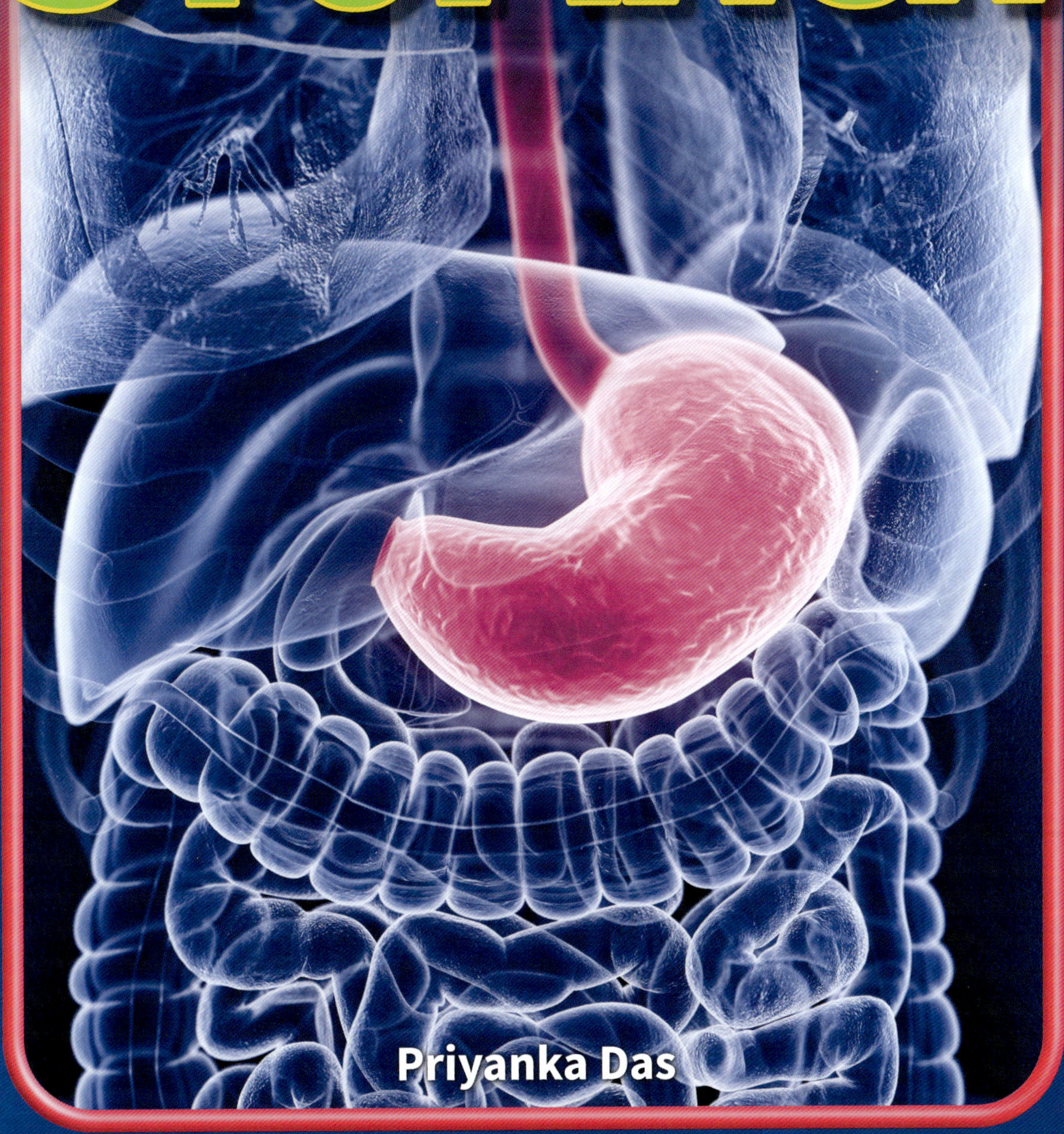

Priyanka Das

LIGHTBOX
openlightbox.com

# LIGHTBOX

Go to
**www.openlightbox.com**
and enter this book's
unique code.

**ACCESS CODE**

**LBXN3522**

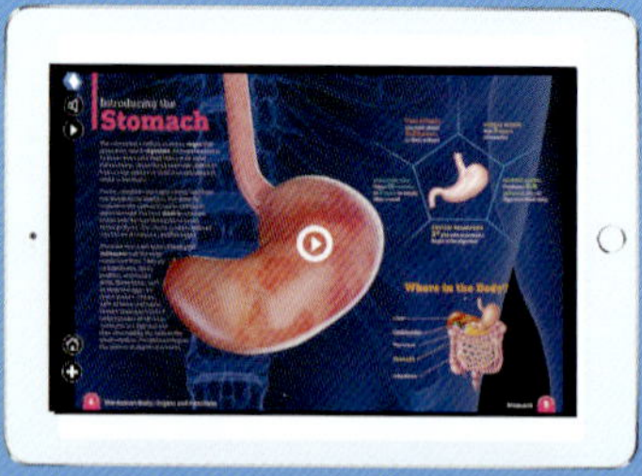

Lightbox is an all-inclusive digital solution for the teaching and learning of curriculum topics in an original, groundbreaking way. Lightbox is based on National Curriculum Standards.

## LIGHTBOX SUPPLEMENTARY RESOURCES

**SHARE**
Share titles within your Learning Management System (LMS) or Library Circulation System

**CURRICULUM**
Find national and state curriculum correlations

**CITATION**
Create bibliographical references following APA, CMOS, and MLA styles

## STANDARD FEATURES OF LIGHTBOX

**AUDIO** High-quality narration using text-to-speech system

**ACTIVITIES** Printable PDFs that can be emailed and graded

**SLIDESHOWS** Pictorial overviews of key concepts

**VIDEOS** Embedded high-definition video clips

**WEBLINKS** Curated links to external, child-safe resources

**TRANSPARENCIES** Step-by-step layering of maps, diagrams, charts, and timelines

**INTERACTIVE MAPS** Interactive maps and aerial satellite imagery

**QUIZZES** Ten multiple-choice questions that are automatically graded and emailed for teacher assessment

**KEY WORDS** Matching key concepts to their definitions

**This title is part of our Lightbox digital subscription**

**Lightbox Grades 6–8 Subscription**
**ISBN 978-1-5105-6068-0**

Access hundreds of Lightbox titles with our digital subscription. Sign up for a **FREE** subscription trial at **www.openlightbox.com/trial**

The digital components of this book are guaranteed to stay active for at least five years from the date of publication.

The Human Body: Organs and Functions

# STOMACH

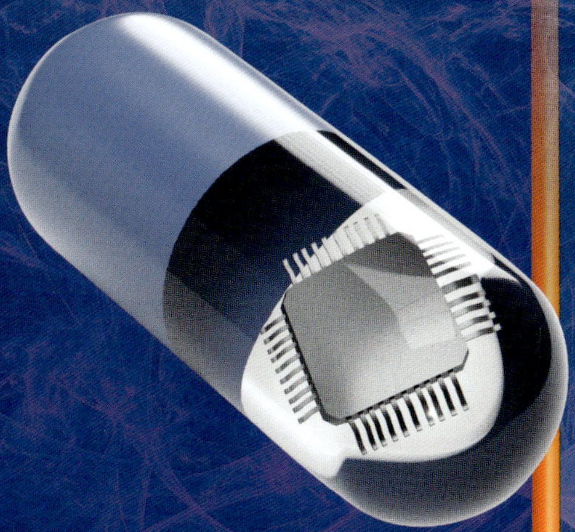

## CONTENTS



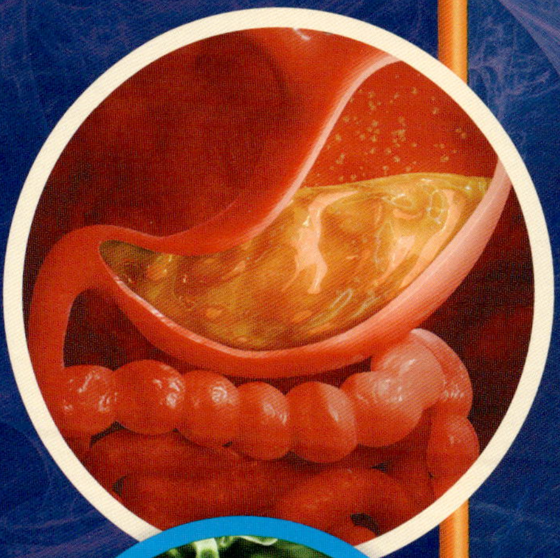

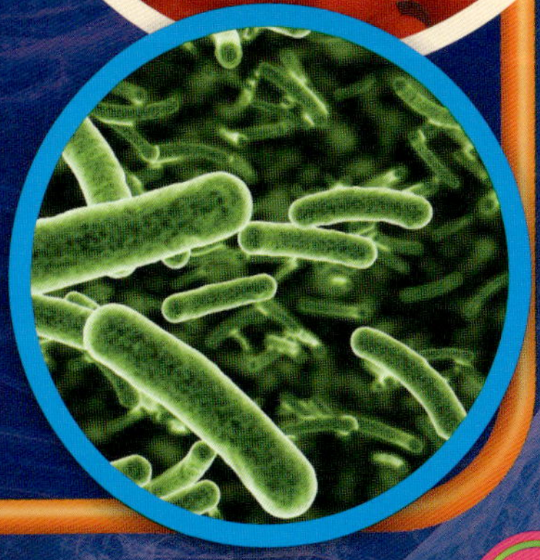

# Introducing the Stomach

The stomach is a hollow, muscular **organ** that plays a key role in **digestion**. Its main function is to break down solid food into a thick liquid called chyme. While the stomach can stretch to hold a large amount of food, it usually empties within a few hours.

A tube called the esophagus carries food from the mouth to the stomach. The powerful muscles in the stomach's walls contract in waves to churn the food. **Gastric** juices are mixed with the food during this process, forming chyme. Chyme is slowly released into the small intestine, another organ.

There are four main types of biological **molecules** that the body needs from food. They are carbohydrates, lipids, proteins, and nucleic acids. Some foods, such as meat and eggs, are rich in protein. Others, such as bread and pasta, contain large quantities of carbohydrates. Most molecules are digested and then absorbed by the body in the small intestine. However, the stomach begins the process of digesting proteins.

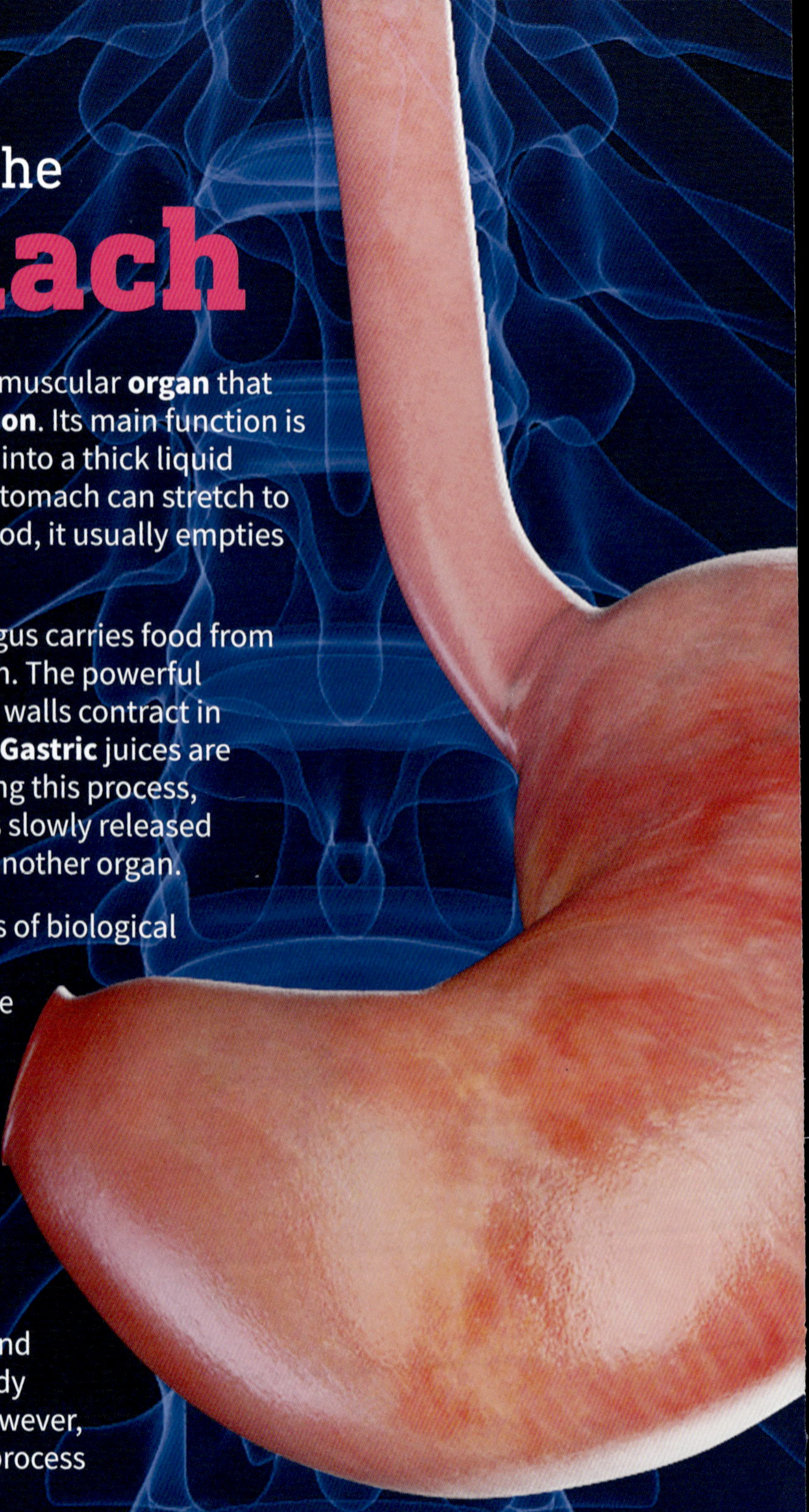

**FOOD STORAGE**
Usually holds about **0.25 gallons** (1 liter) of food when comfortably full

**MUSCLE ACTION**
Has **3 layers** of muscles

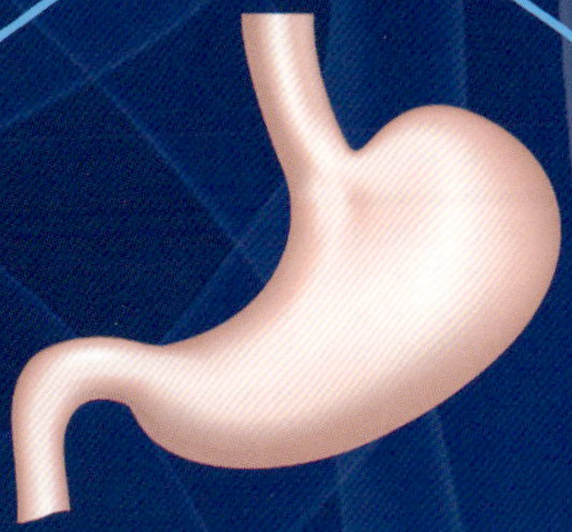

**DIGESTION TIME**
Takes about **40 minutes** to **2 hours** to empty after a meal

**GASTRIC JUICES**
Produces roughly **0.4 gallons** (1.5 L) of digestive fluid each day

**PROTEIN BREAKDOWN**
**1st site** where proteins begin to be digested

## Where in the Body?

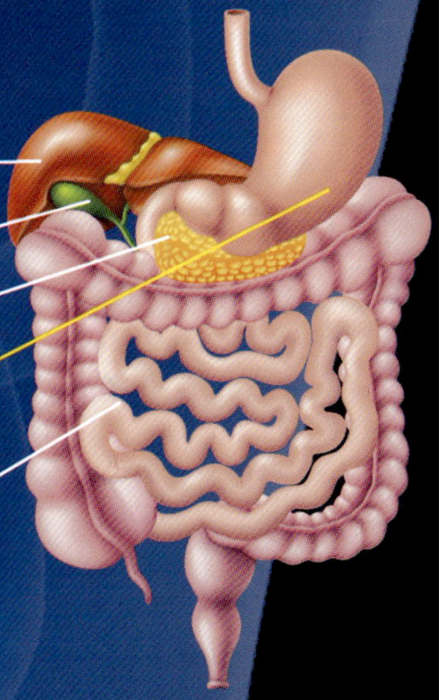

# The Body's Organ Systems

The stomach is part of the digestive system, one of the body's 11 main organ systems. Each organ system performs a specific set of tasks to keep the body healthy and functioning. The digestive system breaks down food, absorbs **nutrients** from it, and removes waste from the body.

The digestive system is primarily made up of a long, connected pathway called the gastrointestinal (GI) tract or digestive tract. It runs from the mouth to the anus. Food travels through the mouth, esophagus, stomach, small intestine, and large intestine before leaving the body. The liver, gallbladder, and pancreas are also part of the digestive system. These organs send substances such as **bile** and **enzymes** into the digestive tract to help break down food.

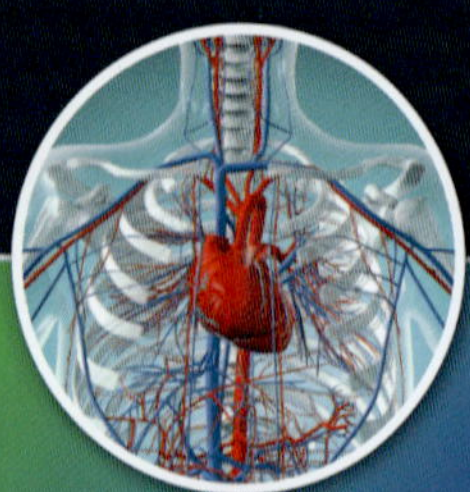

**Circulatory System**
Transports blood, moving substances to and from the body **cells**

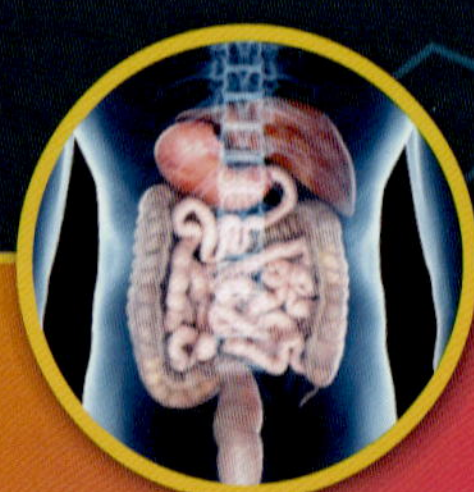

**Digestive System**
Extracts energy and nutrients from food

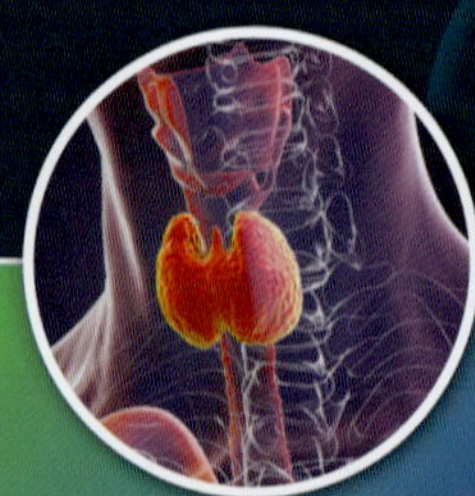

**Endocrine System**
Controls the release of **hormones** and maintains **homeostasis**

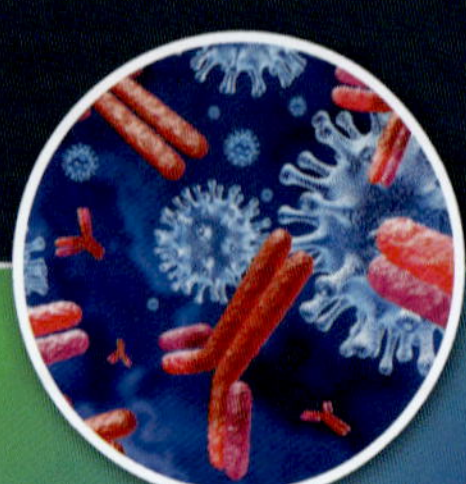

**Immune System**
Protects the body from attack by **pathogens**

**Integumentary System**
Protects the internal organs and is primarily made up of skin

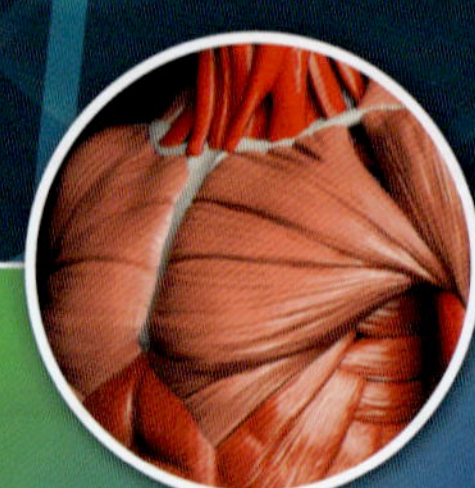

**Muscular System**
Works together with the skeletal system to allow the body to move

Organ systems often work closely together. Once nutrients are absorbed in the small intestine, they enter the bloodstream through small **blood vessels**. The circulatory system then transports these nutrients to the rest of the body.

The nervous system helps direct the digestive system. For example, when people see or smell food, their brain sends signals to tell the stomach to begin digestion. This is why people sometimes begin feeling hungry when they smell food. Endocrine system hormones released by the stomach, such as gastrin, also help regulate digestion.

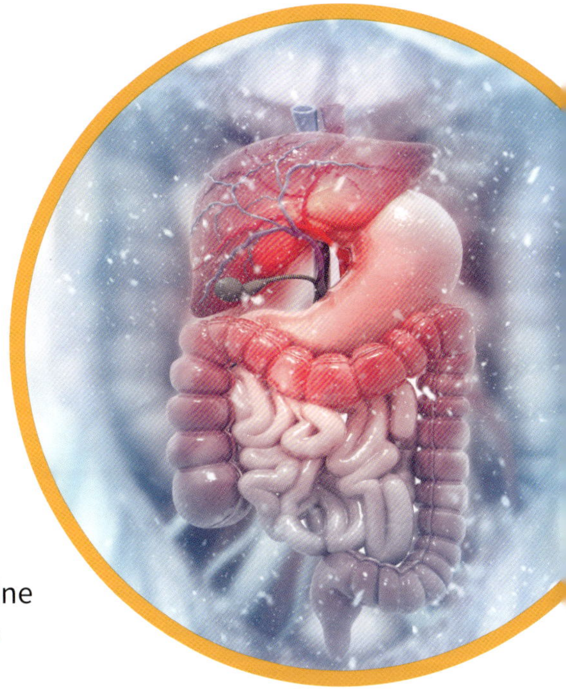

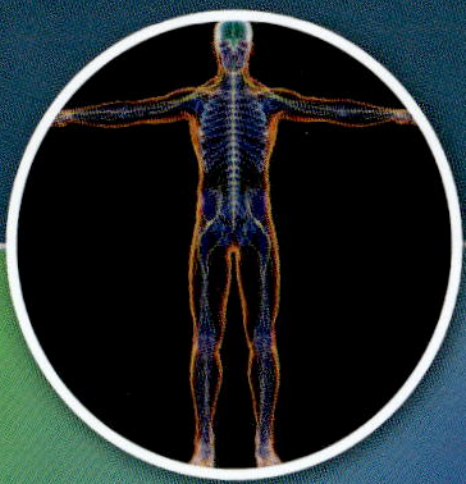

**Nervous System**
Carries signals between the brain and the rest of the body

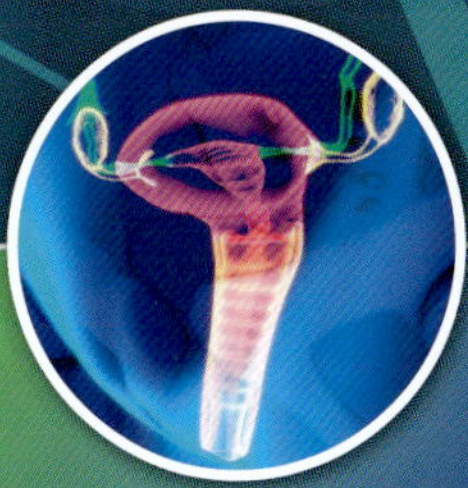

**Reproductive System**
Enables people to have children

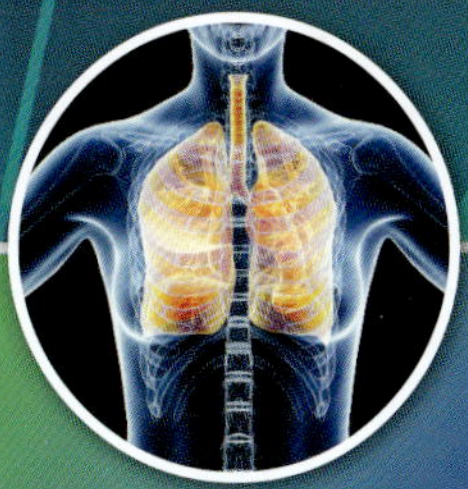

**Respiratory System**
Removes carbon dioxide from the body and takes in oxygen

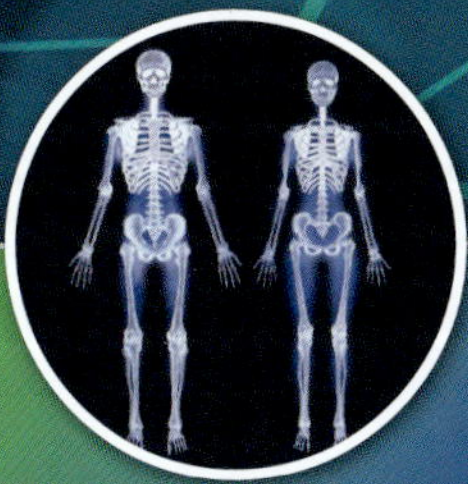

**Skeletal System**
Supports the body and protects the internal organs

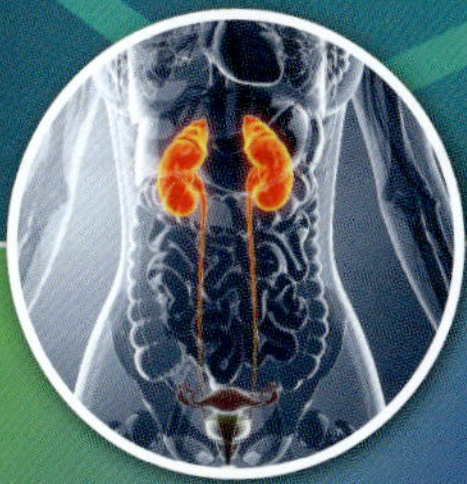

**Urinary System**
Filters blood, removing excess water and some waste products

# Structure of the Stomach

The stomach is located in the upper left **abdomen**. It expands and contracts depending on how much food it contains. The stomach somewhat resembles the letter "J" when empty. As it fills up, it becomes more pear-shaped.

The stomach can be divided into sections. The first part, where food enters from the esophagus, is the cardia. Next is the fundus, a rounded area that stores food and gas. Below this is the body, the largest part. This is where most chyme is formed. The lowest section of the stomach, the pylorus, connects the organ to the small intestine.

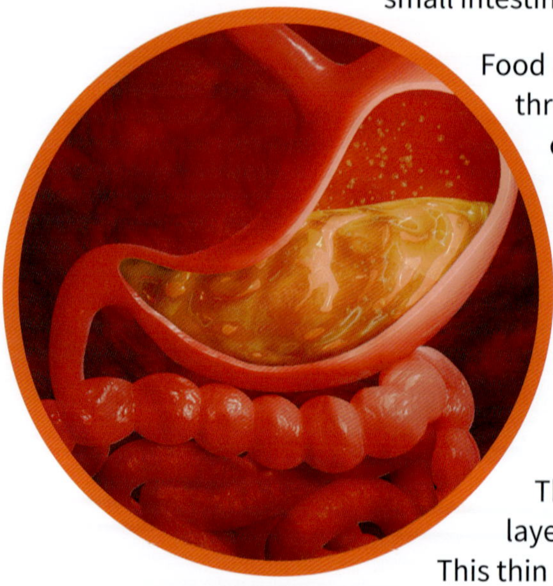

Food enters and leaves the stomach through muscular **valves**. A valve called the lower esophageal sphincter prevents food from moving back into the esophagus. The pyloric sphincter, another valve, controls the release of chyme into the small intestine.

The serosa is the outermost layer of the stomach wall. This thin **membrane** covers and protects the organ. The innermost layer of the stomach is the mucosa. Several types of cells are found in this layer, including parietal and chief cells. Parietal cells produce a strong chemical called hydrochloric acid. Chief cells produce pepsinogen, which becomes an enzyme known as pepsin. This enzyme helps the body digest proteins.

# Digestive Tract

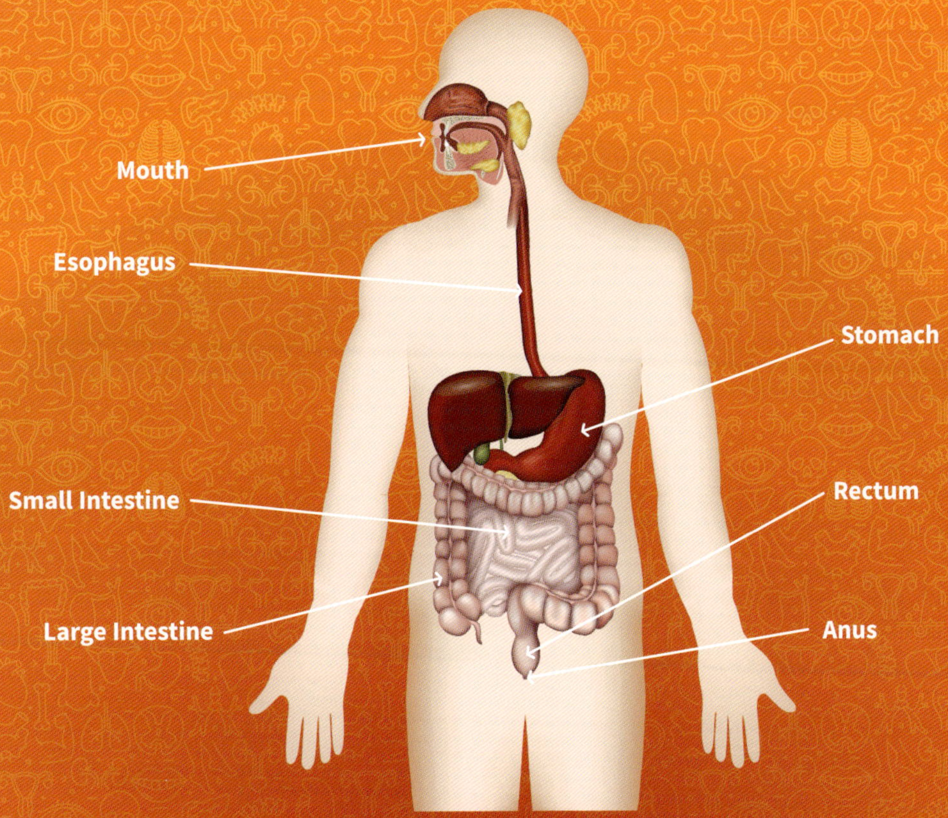


# Stomach Anatomy

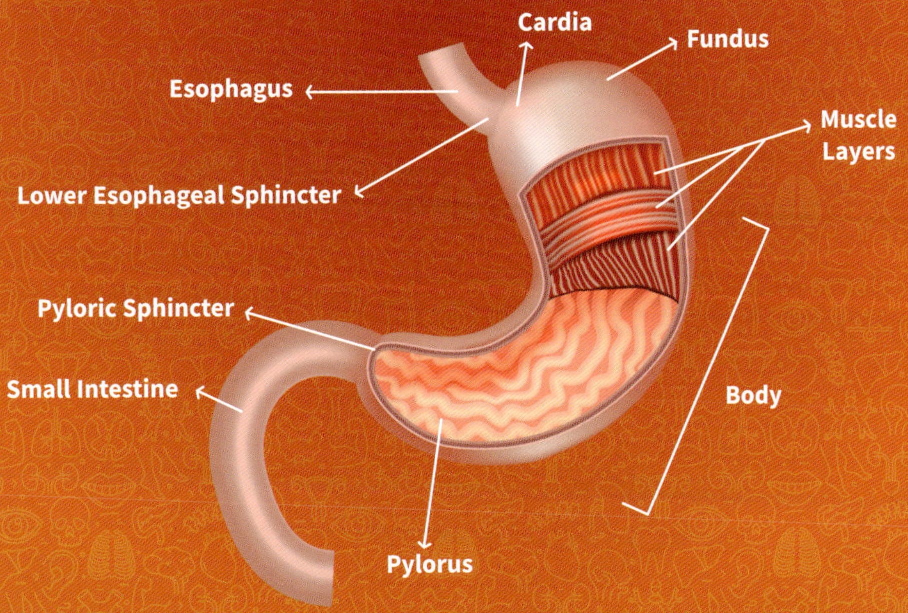

# Role in the Body

Food provides the body with energy. However, food first needs to be broken down into a form that the body is able to use. This is done through two types of digestion that take place in different parts of the GI tract, including the stomach. The stomach also secretes hormones and helps protect the body from harmful substances in food.

## Mechanical Digestion

Mechanical digestion is also known as physical digestion. It involves breaking large pieces of food into smaller pieces using physical movements. Mechanical digestion begins in the mouth and continues in the stomach. To produce chyme, stomach muscles contract in a process called peristalsis. These rhythmic movements churn and mix the food, but do not change it chemically.

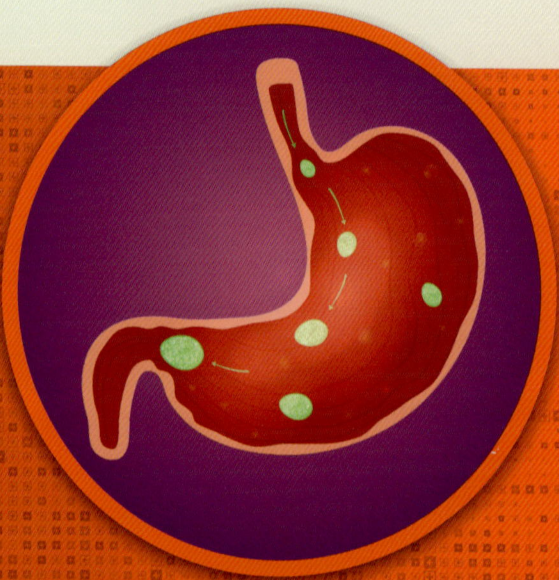

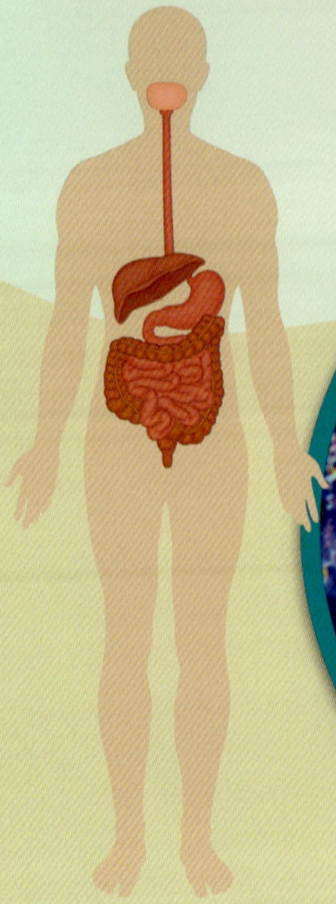

## Chemical Digestion

Chemical digestion changes the chemical structure of food molecules. A small amount of chemical digestion occurs in the stomach. Hydrochloric acid helps create an acidic environment that lets enzymes such as pepsin work effectively. Pepsin breaks proteins into small chains called amino acids, which the body is able to absorb.

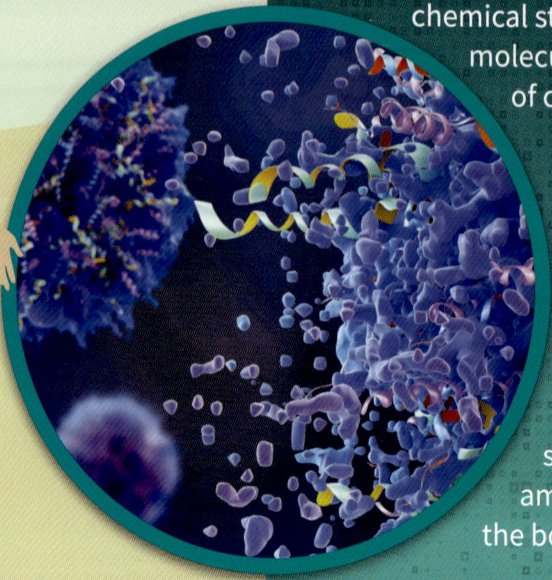

## Defense Against Pathogens

Hydrochloric acid in the stomach kills harmful **bacteria** and other pathogens in food. This reduces the risk of infections entering the body through the digestive system. The stomach's lining protects the rest of the body from the acid's strength, while a thick fluid called mucus helps to protect the lining itself. This allows the stomach to function without harming itself.

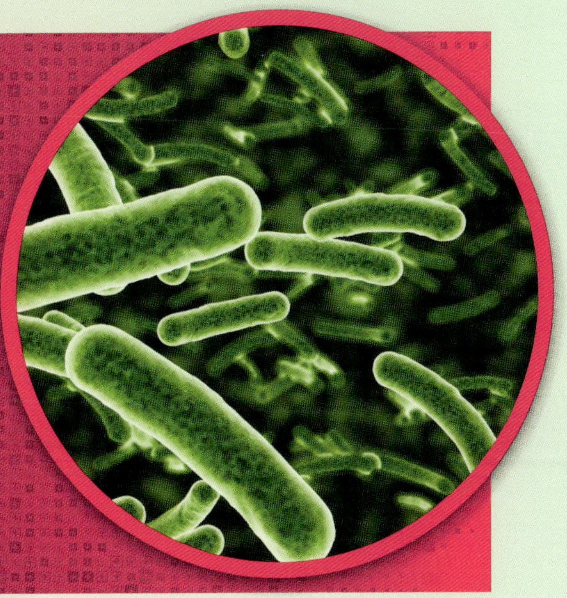

## Hormone Secretion

One of the main hormones released by the stomach is gastrin. It signals parietal cells to produce more hydrochloric acid when food is present. Gastrin also helps control the movement of food through the digestive tract. Ghrelin, the "hunger hormone," is released by the stomach as well. It increases appetite.

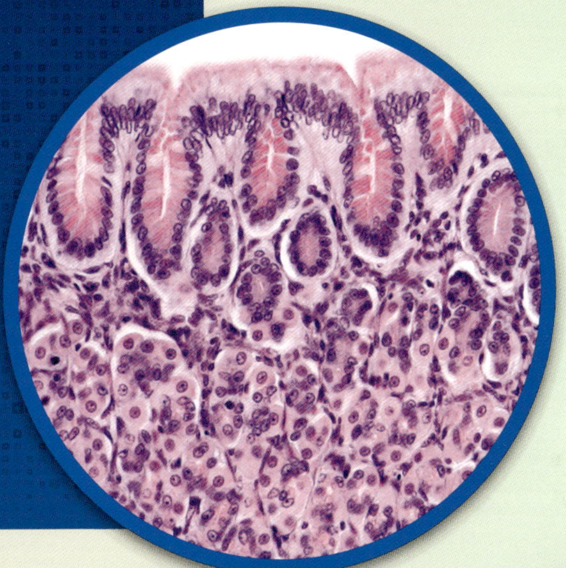

### Can You Live Without It? YES!

While it is possible to live without a stomach, doing so requires major lifestyle changes. In certain cases, the stomach may need to be surgically removed due to diseases, such as stomach cancer. This procedure is known as a gastrectomy. It can be partial or total. After a total gastrectomy, the esophagus is connected directly to the small intestine. People without a stomach must eat smaller, more frequent meals. They typically need supplements to replace certain **micronutrients** that are no longer absorbed efficiently.

# A Medical Timeline

Ancient physicians noted the effects of digestion and stomach pain, while modern scientists have studied the stomach's chemical functions and disorders in detail. Developments over time have helped shape the field of gastroenterology. The name comes from the Greek words *gastro*, or "stomach," *entero*, or "intestine," and *logia*, or "study."

**circa 1600 BC**

The **Edwin Smith papyrus**, an ancient Egyptian medical text, describes how the stomach and some other organs work.

**circa 400 BC**

Ancient Greek physician **Hippocrates** links diet and stomach health. He writes about the effects of improper digestion.

**circa 200 AD**

In Rome, the physician **Galen** believes that the stomach is capable of sensing when it is empty and creating the sensation of hunger in response.

**circa 1500**

Italian artist and scholar Leonardo da Vinci sketches **detailed drawings** of the digestive system. He also describes its workings, including how the stomach muscles contract.

**1833**

U.S. army surgeon **William Beaumont** publishes a study describing how digestion is a chemical process in addition to a mechanical one.

**1836**

Theodor Schwann, a German **physiologist**, **discovers pepsin**.

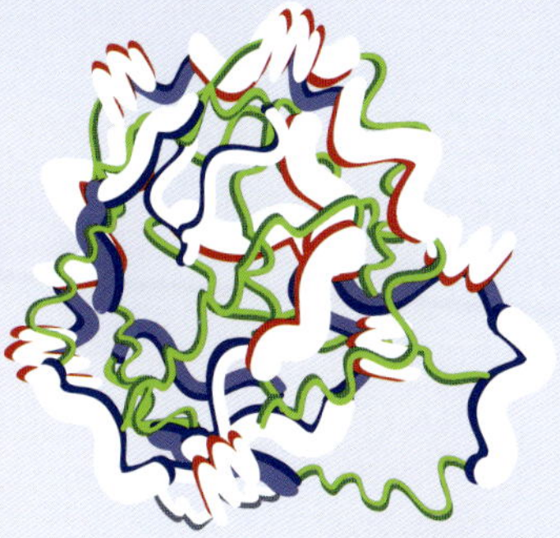

**1982**

Australian scientists Barry Marshall and Robin Warren discover that the ***Helicobacter pylori*** *(H. pylori)* bacteria can cause stomach **ulcers**.

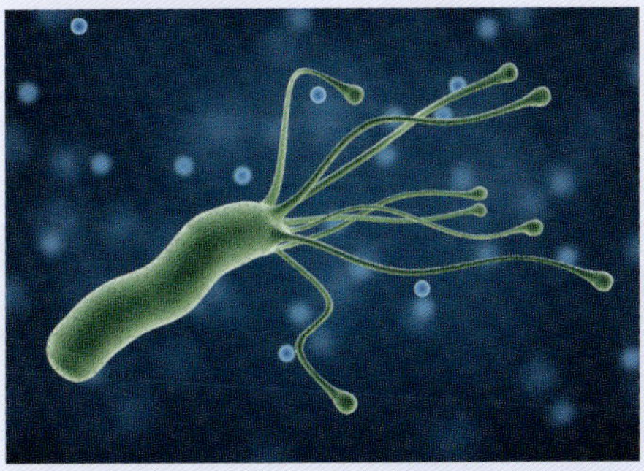

**1994**

The **World Health Organization (WHO)** classifies *H. pylori* as a major cause of stomach cancer.

**2001**

Advancements in technology allow doctors to use a **small pill camera** swallowed by a patient to see inside the stomach.

**2025**

The 20th Euro-Global Gastroenterology Conference is held in Zurich, Switzerland, to discuss **advances in gastroenterology**.

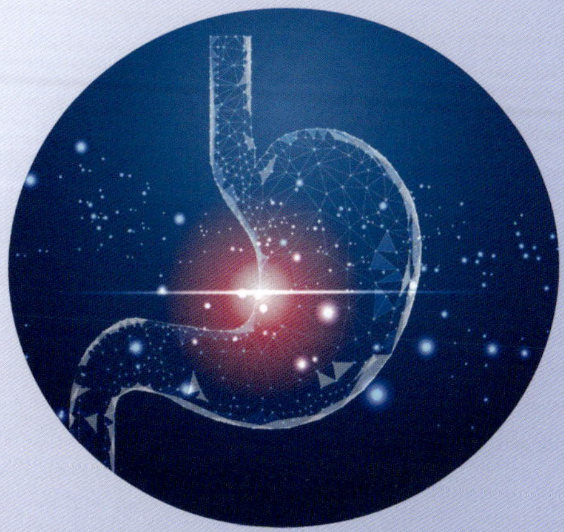

# Organs Working Together

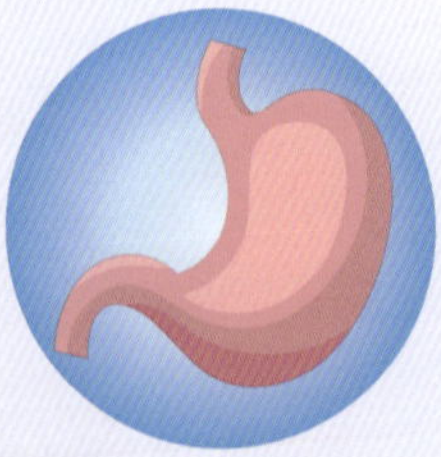

Part of the stomach's role in the digestive process is to work with other key organs. Together, they make digestion more efficient. Mechanical digestion increases the surface area of food, which gives enzymes more sites to work on. This speeds up chemical digestion.

## The Stomach works with the...

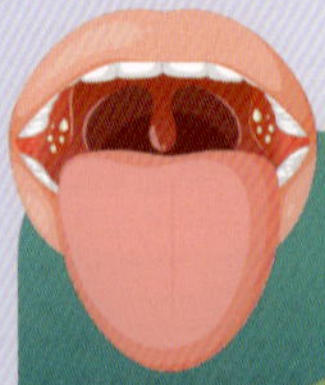

### **Mouth**, which Begins Digestion

1. Teeth and saliva in mouth begin breaking down food
2. Food forms a ball called a bolus
3. Bolus moves down esophagus through peristalsis
4. Bolus enters stomach through lower esophageal sphincter

### **Small Intestine**, which Absorbs Nutrients

1. Stomach sends chyme into small intestine through pyloric sphincter
2. Enzymes and bile complete digestion
3. Nutrients are absorbed into bloodstream
4. Blood vessels transport nutrients around body

## Brain, which Helps Regulate Digestion

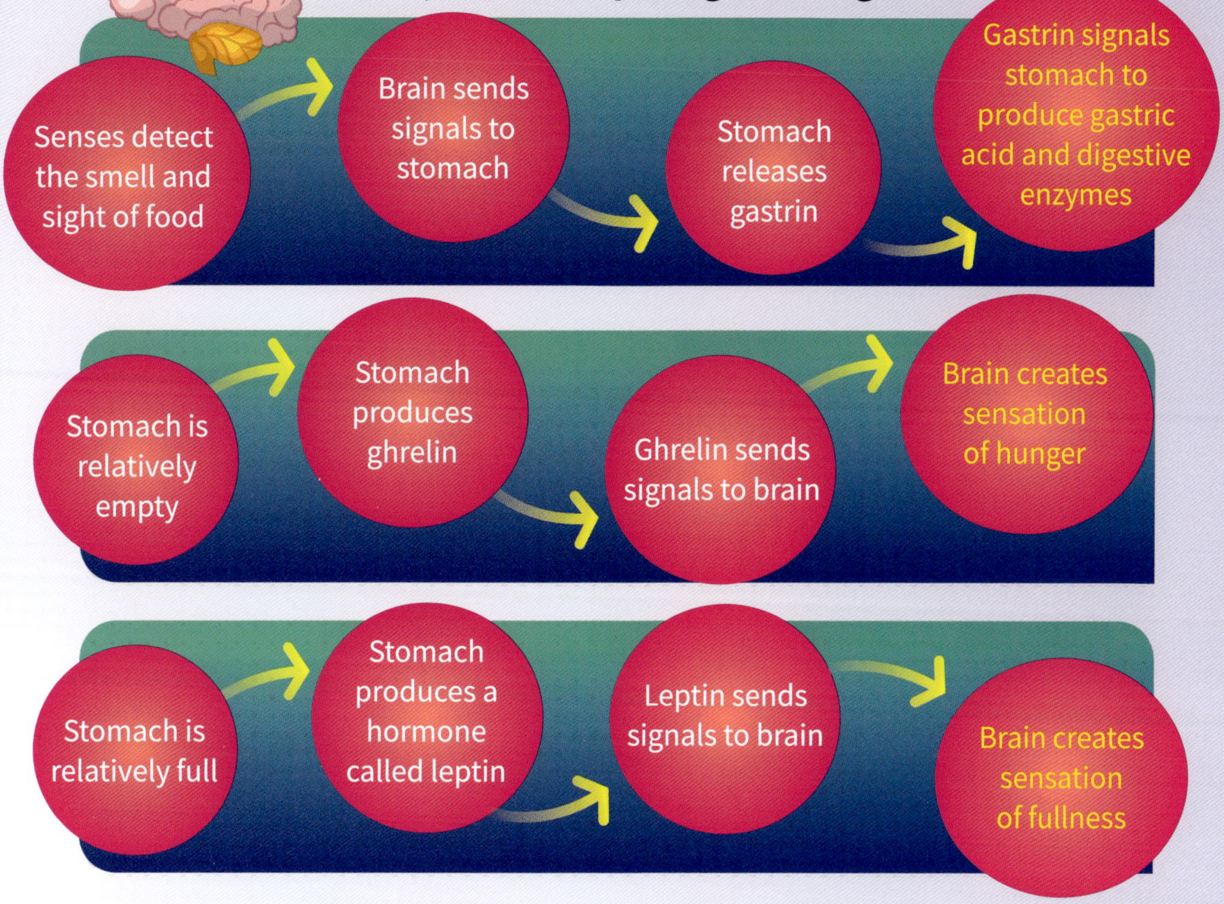


## Pancreas, which Secretes Enzymes

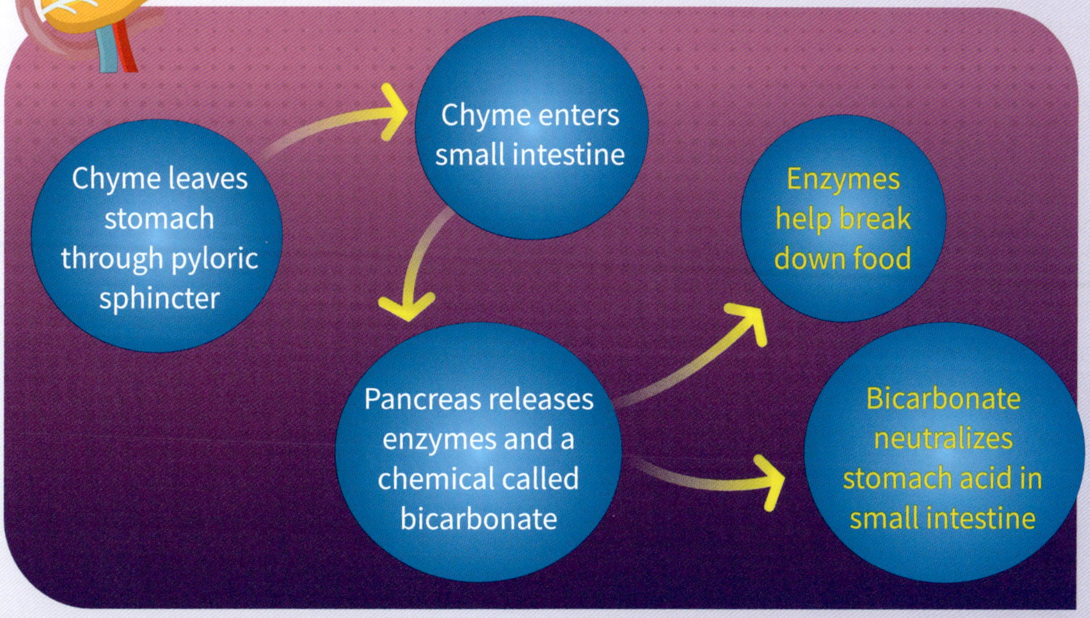

# Diseases of the Stomach

Many medical conditions affect how the stomach functions. They can interfere with digestion and cause pain. In some cases, they may lead to serious complications. Stomach diseases include gastritis, ulcers, gastroesophageal reflux disease (GERD), and stomach cancer.

## Gastritis

Gastritis is an **inflammation** of the stomach lining that protects the organ from the acids and enzymes inside it. Stomach pain, bloating, nausea, and vomiting are some possible symptoms of gastritis. This condition may be caused by infection, medications, or stress. Acute gastritis is sudden and temporary, while chronic gastritis is a long-lasting disease.

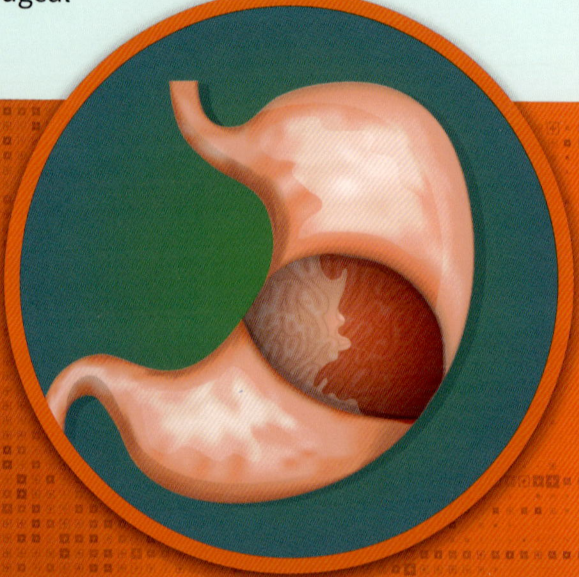

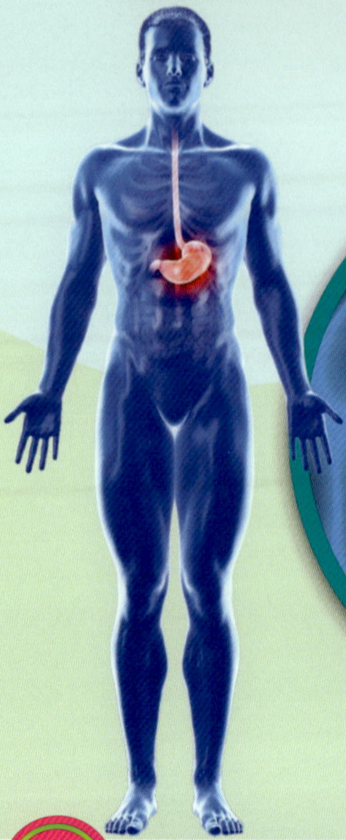

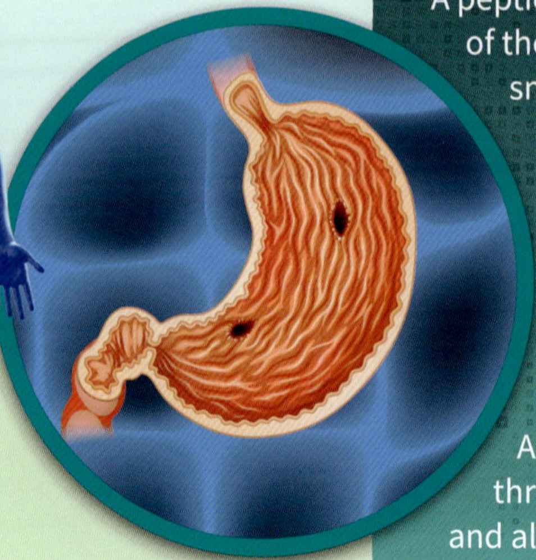

## Stomach Ulcers

A peptic ulcer is an open sore in the lining of the stomach or upper part of the small intestine. Stomach ulcers occur when the acids inside the stomach eat through the organ's lining. They are often caused by *H. pylori* or long-term use of certain drugs. If untreated, peptic ulcers can bleed or develop into perforated ulcers.

A perforated ulcer is a hole that goes through all the layers of the stomach and allows its acidic contents to leak out into the abdominal cavity.

## Gastroesophageal Reflux Disease

GERD occurs when stomach acid flows back up into the esophagus. This happens due to a weakened lower esophageal sphincter. GERD leads to symptoms such as heartburn, chest discomfort, and a sour taste in the mouth. Long-term GERD can damage the lining of the esophagus.

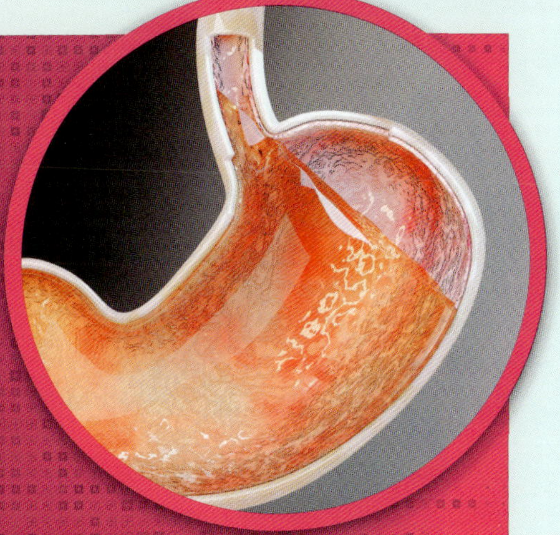

## Stomach Cancer

Also known as gastric cancer, stomach cancer occurs when abnormal cells grow in the stomach lining. The growth then spreads to the walls of the stomach. Stomach cancer may develop slowly and is often difficult to detect in its early stages. Risk factors include *H. pylori*, smoking, and a family history of stomach cancer.

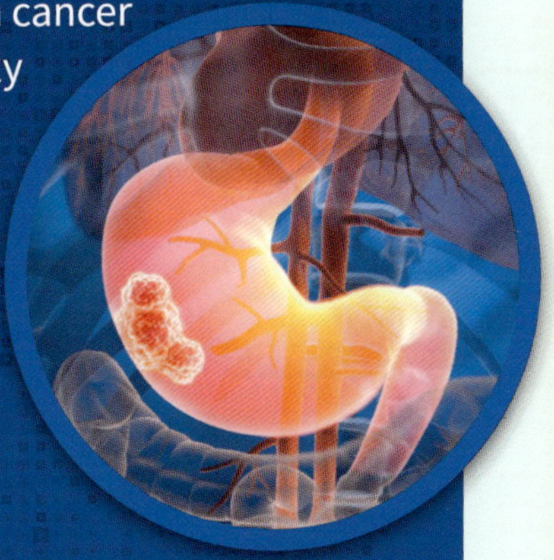

## Warning Signs!

Certain symptoms may point to stomach problems. If these signs appear, it is important to go and see a doctor.

- Ongoing stomach pain or discomfort
- Nausea or frequent vomiting
- Feeling bloated or full after small meals
- Loss of appetite
- Black or bloody stools
- Unexplained weight loss
- Indigestion

## *Helicobacter pylori*

The *H. pylori* bacteria is one of the main causes of stomach problems around the world. It often infects people through contaminated food or water. By attacking the stomach's protective lining, an *H. pylori* infection can cause gastritis. Left untreated, it can lead to peptic ulcers over time. Long-term infection may also increase the risk of stomach cancer.

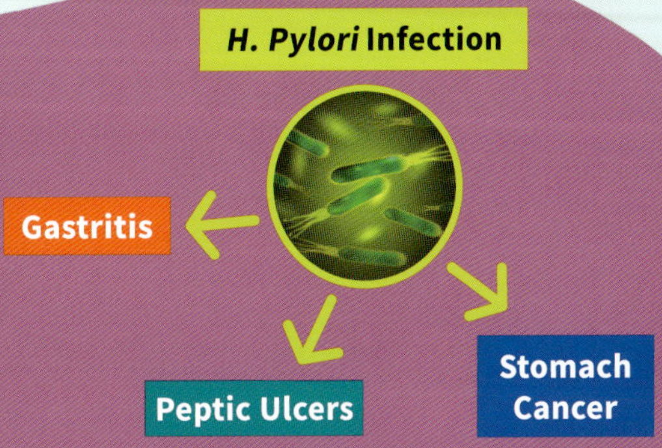

# Medicine around the World

Gastroenterology departments in hospitals around the world focus on treating stomach diseases. Many research centers also study conditions that affect the stomach and the rest of the digestive tract. Scientists and doctors work to find new ways to treat or prevent stomach conditions such as infections, ulcers, and cancer.

## Mayo Clinic, United States

1

The Mayo Clinic's campus in Rochester, Minnesota, has one of the largest gastroenterology departments in the world. It offers advanced care for patients with GERD, ulcers, and stomach cancer. Researchers at the Mayo Clinic work on improving **endoscopy** technology and drug treatments.

## Karolinska Institute, Sweden

2

Located in Stockholm, the Karolinska Institute is known for its digestive health research. Its scientists study how gut bacteria interact with vaccines and other drugs. The institute has made contributions to the understanding of *H. pylori* and other bacteria in the stomach, including how childhood infections may influence lifelong gastric health.

## Agostino Gemelli University Policlinic, Italy

3

Rome's Agostino Gemelli University Policlinic is one of Italy's leading hospitals for gastroenterology and stomach cancer care. Its specialists use endoscopy and advanced diagnostic tools to treat a wide range of stomach conditions, including *H. pylori* infection, gastritis, and peptic ulcers. Researchers at Gemelli also study factors that affect stomach cancer.

## Kyoto University Hospital, Japan

4

Japan has a high rate of stomach cancer. Researchers at Kyoto University Hospital study the genetic and environmental factors behind this trend. The hospital conducts studies on early cancer detection and prevention strategies. It also trains specialists in advanced gastrointestinal surgery techniques.

### What is a Gastroenterologist?

Doctors who specialize in the digestive tract are called gastroenterologists. They treat conditions involving the stomach, intestines, and other related organs. A gastroenterologist uses tools such as endoscopes to examine the stomach. Gastroenterologists also perform procedures and provide care for patients with chronic digestive conditions.

# Keeping the Stomach Healthy

There are many ways to protect the stomach and keep the digestive system functioning well. Healthy habits from a young age support long-term stomach health. These include eating properly, managing stress, and avoiding harmful substances.

TIP 1

**Eat Balanced Meals**

Eating fruits, vegetables, whole grains, and lean proteins provides the stomach with food it can easily digest. Eating slowly and chewing food thoroughly also reduces strain on the stomach.

TIP 2

**Limit Spicy and Acidic Foods**

Foods high in spice or acid can irritate the stomach lining, especially in people with digestive disorders or sensitive stomachs.

TIP 3

**Avoid Overeating**

Large meals stretch the stomach and increase acid production. Eating small, frequent meals helps the stomach handle digestion more easily.

TIP 4

**Reduce Stress**

Emotional stress can affect digestion. Practicing relaxation techniques such as deep breathing, yoga, or meditation may help regulate the stomach's functions.

TIP 5

**Practice Good Hygiene**

Washing hands before eating and preparing food safely reduces the chance of infection. Proper hygiene helps prevent *H. pylori* and other harmful bacteria from entering the digestive system.

# Activity: Digestion in a Bag

Your stomach breaks down food using strong muscles and acidic digestive juices. Using a plastic bag and some food, you can get a rough idea of how different types of food are mixed, mashed, and dissolved inside your body.

**Materials**

- Clear, sealable plastic bags
- Water
- Vinegar
- Slice of bread
- Banana
- Crackers

**Steps**

**1. Smell the Food:** Do you notice anything happening inside your mouth? Seeing or smelling food often causes saliva, or spit, to form.

**2. Rip It Up:** Take half a slice of bread. Use your fingers to tear it into smaller pieces. This represents what happens when your teeth chew food in your mouth.

**3. Add the Food:** Open the plastic bag and put the pieces of bread inside it. The plastic bag represents your stomach.

**4. Add Water:** Pour about 2 tablespoons of water into the plastic bag and then seal it.

**5. Squish and Squeeze:** Make sure the bag is sealed tightly. Then, gently squeeze the bag with your hands. This mimics how the stomach muscles churn and mash food to break it down. Continue squishing for one minute and observe what happens.

**6. Observe the Changes:** Open the bag slightly and take a careful look. What does the food look like now? Has it changed shape, texture, or size? Write down your observations.

**7. Adding Acid:** Repeat Steps 1 to 4 with the remaining bread. After Step 4, add 1 tablespoon of vinegar to the bag. This will act as a weaker version of hydrochloric acid. You can then continue on with Steps 5 and 6.

**8. Changing the Food:** Repeat Steps 1 to 7 with the banana. Then, repeat them again with the crackers. You can also try doing this with other types of food.

**9. Discuss Your Observations:** Did the food break down faster with just water or with the combination of water and vinegar? Which food broke down the fastest and which took the longest? Discuss what you observed and what this has taught you about the stomach. Consider why some foods are digested more easily than others and what this might mean for a person's diet.

# Quiz

**1**
What is the main function of the stomach?

**2**
Which letter of the alphabet does the stomach resemble when empty?

**3**
Name the two types of digestion that occur in the body.

**4**
Who discovered the enzyme pepsin?

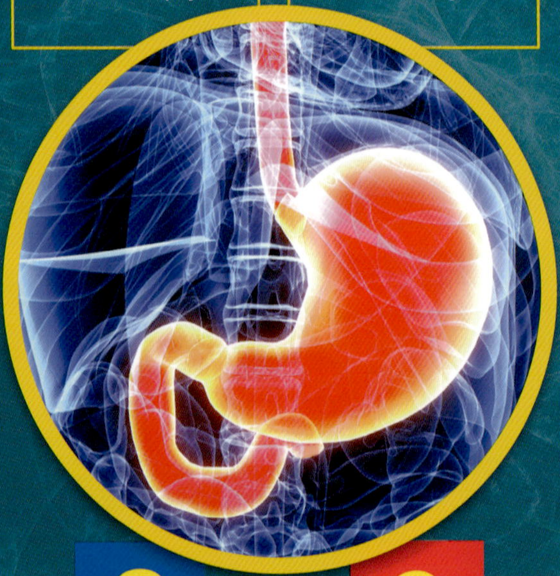

**5**
What is another name for the digestive tract?

**6**
When does the stomach produce the hormone ghrelin?

**7**
Which bacteria is one of the main causes of stomach problems around the world?

**8**
Which valve connects the stomach to the small intestine?

**9**
What is gastritis?

**10**
Which strong chemical is produced by parietal cells?

**ANSWERS**

**1.** To break down solid food into a thick liquid called chyme **2.** The letter "J" **3.** Mechanical digestion and chemical digestion **4.** Theodor Schwann **5.** Gastrointestinal tract **6.** When it is relatively empty **7.** *Helicobacter pylori* **8.** Pyloric sphincter **9.** Inflammation of the stomach lining **10.** Hydrochloric acid

# Key Words

**abdomen:** the part of the body that is located between the chest and pelvis and contains the digestive organs

**bacteria:** tiny organisms that can cause diseases

**bile:** a greenish-yellow digestive fluid that helps break down fats

**blood vessels:** tubes that carry blood throughout the body

**cells:** the smallest structural and functional units of living organisms

**digestion:** the process of breaking down food into smaller parts that the body can absorb

**endoscopy:** a medical test that uses a thin, flexible tube with a camera to look inside the digestive tract

**enzymes:** special types of proteins that speed up chemical reactions, such as the chemical digestion of food

**gastric:** related to the stomach

**homeostasis:** the body's ability to maintain a stable internal environment despite external changes

**hormones:** chemical messengers that affect many functions in the body

**inflammation:** the body's response to injury or infection, often resulting in redness, swelling, heat, or pain

**membrane:** a thin layer of tissue that covers or lines parts of the body

**micronutrients:** substances that the body needs in very small amounts, such as vitamins and minerals

**molecules:** the smallest unit of a substance

**nutrients:** substances in food that the body uses for energy, growth, and repair

**organ:** a distinct structure in the body that is made up of tissues and performs one or more specific functions

**pathogens:** microorganisms, such as bacteria or viruses, that cause diseases

**physiologist:** a scientist who studies how the organs and systems of the body work

**ulcers:** open sores formed by breaks in the skin or the lining of an organ

**valves:** structures that control the flow of food and fluids in the body by opening and closing

# Index

# LIGHTBOX

## SUPPLEMENTARY RESOURCES

Click on the plus icon ⊕ found in the bottom left corner of each spread to open additional teacher resources.

- Download and print the book's quizzes and activities
- Access curriculum correlations
- Explore additional web applications that enhance the Lightbox experience

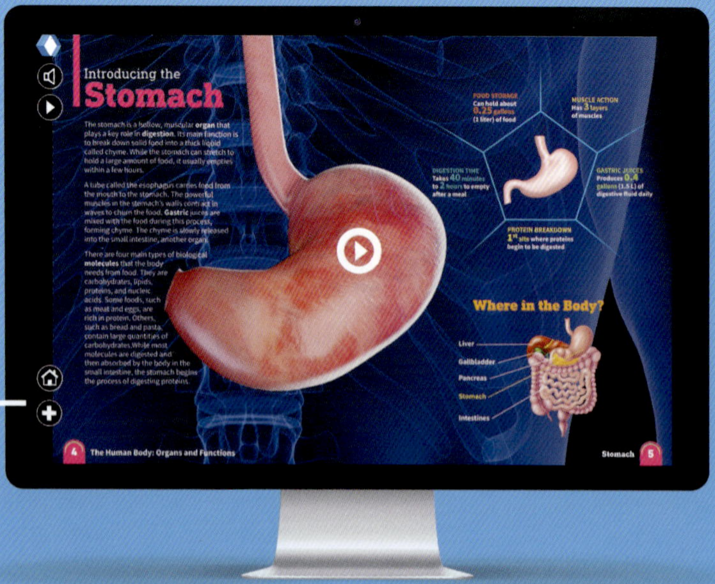


## LIGHTBOX DIGITAL TITLES
### Packed full of integrated media

**VIDEOS**

**INTERACTIVE MAPS**

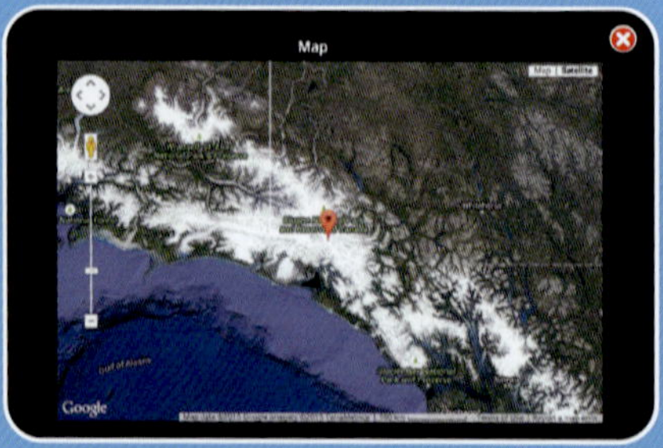


**WEBLINKS**

**SLIDESHOWS**

**QUIZZES**

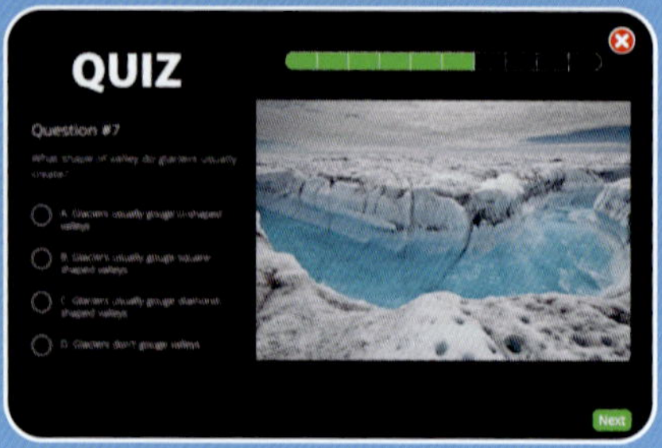


## OPTIMIZED FOR

- ✓ TABLETS
- ✓ SMART BOARDS
- ✓ COMPUTERS
- ✓ AND MUCH MORE!

Published by Lightbox Learning Inc.
276 5th Avenue, Suite 704 #917
New York, NY 10001
Website: www.openlightbox.com



Library of Congress Control Number: 2025932679

ISBN 978-1-5105-8701-4 (hardcover)
ISBN 978-1-5105-8702-1 (static multi-user eBook)
ISBN 978-1-5105-8704-5 (interactive multi-user eBook)

Printed in Fargo, North Dakota, in the United States of America
2 3 4 5 6 7 8 9 0 30 29 28 27 26

012026
260119

**Project Coordinator:** Priyanka Das
**Design:** Jean Faye Rodriguez

The publisher has made every reasonable effort to trace ownership and to obtain permission to use copyright material. The publisher would be pleased to have any errors or omissions brought to its attention so that they may be corrected in subsequent printings. Some visual elements in this title may have been generated using AI. While we strive for accuracy in all aspects of our products, we cannot guarantee that the elements depicted in these images are accurate. The publisher acknowledges Getty Images, Shutterstock, Wikimedia, and Flux as the primary image suppliers for this title. If you have any inquiries about these images or would like to provide any feedback, please reach out to us at feedback@openlightbox.com

All of the Internet URLs and Google Maps links given in the interactive eBook were valid at the time of publication. However, due to the dynamic nature of the Internet, some addresses may have changed, or sites may have ceased to exist since publication. While the author and publisher regret any inconvenience this may cause readers, no responsibility for any such changes can be accepted by either the author or the publisher.